Life
with the
Guru

ART HOCHBERG

Kalima Publishing
Philadelphia, Pennsylvania

Library of Congress Control Number: 2014920025

Life with the Guru
Art Hochberg, Kalima Publishing. 2014
p. cm.
Trade paperback
ISBN 13: 978-0-9888075-5-6
1. Self-Help. 2. Existential Psychology. 3. Spirituality. 4. Wisdom. 5. Healing.

"A Dr. Art Book"

His friends call him "Dr. Art." With incisive wit and style of a Zen master the good doctor offers patience, gratitude and the determination to be all right with ourselves. In Life with the Guru, Dr. Art shares the story of his experiences with Guru Bawa and how they serve to transform his life.

Trade eBook ISBN: 978-0-9888075-5-6

Cover Illustration/Design by Michael Green

Book typography by Didona Design

Dr. Art, "Letting Go!" photo by Greg Robinson.

Table of Contents

Dedicated to

M. R. BAWA MUHAIYADDEEN

A genuine Sufi Master

M. R. BAWA MUHAIYADDEEN

Introduction

Life with the Guru is a book about my journey with the Guru, M.R. Bawa Muhaiyaddeen. What I want to share with the readers are some of the very special stories and anecdotes that have come to be as a result of my being with him. This is my personal story. Take what you want from it.

The thing about the relationship with the Guru is that it is endless. The point for us to see is that within the reality of our lives there is that aspect that is never ending. But, really that's a kind of faith that can give us great determination and gratitude.

The key is that the Guru, Bawa, did not know anything at all. He was a slave of the Creator. He held the highest position that could be held as a slave. Bawa said to us, "Take whatever I say and use your wisdom," which meant that we had a choice as to whether what he was saying related to us at that particular time. To me, this was the essence of the way Bawa taught.

The main teaching that Bawa gave us was that there was only the Zikr, which in Arabic is la ilaha illAllahu, which essentially means, "I do not exist; only God exists." It is our breath that is attached to the Zikr. This was the practice that he taught us and the true Zikr is said silently.

So what is the point of telling these stories about the

Guru? The point is that these stories are designed to show us that anything's possible. It expands our experience of what can happen.

The aphorisms I have written at the end of each story are further reflections on this point.

> *"Things may make sense at the time we do them. Then later on, they may make absolutely no sense at all. Isn't that amazing? Actually often they don't make any sense even while we're doing them."*

The Way to America

Before Bawa came to America he was really ill. He had several doctors around him. Now several days before, Bawa had received an invitation from several Fellowship people to come to America. He had never been there before. At this point, Bawa had no strength and stayed in bed all the time. His physical condition was getting worse, and on one particular day he actually passed away. The doctors were sitting around him and noticed no vital signs. The Ceylonese all began to wail and cry that Bawa had passed. After about five minutes or so, he sat upright in his bed and said, "Well, I guess we're going to America." This story was related to me by Dr. Marker who was present in Ceylon at the time and he related it to me several months later.

"Everyone has their own life to lead, in their own way. You know, when you really look at things as they appear, the whole trip is simply unbelievable. Actually, it's totally ridiculous most of the time."

"Live every day as if it were your last. Life can be amazing or confusing. No need to take a bruising, or think you're losing. Just keep cruising and amusing."

"It's better sometimes to not expect something to happen. Often the expecting is what keeps it from happening. Give up expecting anything to happen. That clears the way for happening or not happening."

"It may seem that we have multiple realities— because we're capable of playing many different roles in our life."

"At any given moment you might as well give as much love as you can. Why be stingy with it? You owe it to yourself."

Meeting the Guru

In April 1973, I met the Guru. I knew he was the Guru because he was ancient to me. I was looking for an ancient man to learn wisdom from. I knew immediately that my life was going to change very fast and it did.

The first thing that he said that totally struck me was that the world is a university. Now to me, that was my experience that the world was a university. Everything that Bawa said to us that made a big impact on us were things that we already knew. This was just playing out an aspect of me that I needed to totally bring up and be.

"Everyone here now is going to die – but really no one knows what death is really like. Maybe we just take on another part in this never-ending play of life as it unfolds. There is no end to the journey."

"Really, when you think about it – how can God speak through everybody? Hmmmmmm."

"What you experience is your reality, for the time being anyway. It's a mind-blower because, at a certain level of awareness, that's not real either."

"Time does not pass – only events pass and where do they go? Hmmmmmm."

"You have as many burdens on your shoulders as you choose to place there."

Bawa and the Zen Robes

About six months after I met Bawa, I had decided that this wasn't for me. I was going to take off. Now I had been living at a Zen Buddhist temple and had now become part of Bawa's entourage. I had decided I would leave and work on an Indian reservation in South Dakota as a professor at the Indian college, which at the time was the only Indian college in the United States.

So, I went and accepted the position to go and work on the reservation. First, I went to visit the Zen Master at the Buddhist temple and I bid him goodbye. I told him what I was going to do with the Indians and he said, "That's good, you set up a place of meditation there." Then he gave me some very fancy robes and a gold bib. So in a sense, he was initiating me as a Zen Master. He wrapped up these robes and bid me goodbye.

I had a VW bus at the time and I put the robes in the VW bus and went to see the Guru. He was sitting on his bed, and there was a translator at his side. I told the translator that I was going to South Dakota. Bawa looked at me. I cannot describe the look he gave me. He shook his head and said no. Still I wanted to go, so I headed down to the VW bus to take off. I get in the bus and the bus won't start. Not only will the bus not start, but now the robes were gone. The bus was locked and it looked like there was no attempt by anyone to enter the bus.

So I thought for awhile and went back up to see the Guru and said to the translator, "Can you ask Bawa why I shouldn't leave and go to South Dakota?" I believe he thought that I wanted to go to South Dakota because I wanted to just wander around and be a hippie, but he didn't say that. He said, "Don't go to South Dakota. The water is bad. You'll get sick. Stay here with me, it will be better." So I accepted what he said, and I called the people in South Dakota and said that my Guru said I should not leave.

It was helpful of course that there was a mystery that the VW bus didn't start and that my Zen robes were gone. Years later I asked Bawa, "Did you take my Zen robes?" He just smiled.

"The trip is to play your part in the play knowing all along that you are not the one playing the part. That requires a good dose of faith and another dose of exquisite humor– sort of like looking in the mirror. Who is that?"

"Original sin ... the big lie."

"At some point we have to be able to say, "I have no idea what is going on." Hmmmmmmmm. I wonder if that's the whole trip, so that we can actually know what's going on. Hmmmmmmmm."

"Don't overplay your part– underplay your part. That's the way to play it effectively."

"There is no time– everything's going on at the same time. How does that work?"

Surrender to the Guru

In December 1973, I had been with Bawa for about eight months by then, and I realized that I was going to take off unless I could get married and settle down. So I told this to Bawa and asked him if he would find me a wife. He said, "Alright, you look around and see if there's anybody you like, and I'll look around."

So about a month passed, and I had pretty much forgotten about it. Then one day, I came to the Fellowship and someone said to me, "Bawa wants to see you in his room," which was upstairs. I walked into the room and there was a marriage already taking place between two other people. Bawa was marrying them because they had requested it. I walked into the room and saw what was happening and I went to the back to try to just meld in with the surroundings.

Well, he called my name and I went up to see him. He asked me if I still wanted to get married, and I said yes. He asked, "Do you trust me to pick somebody out for you?" I responded, "Yes." Then he called up one of the Fellowship girls, named Anne, and had her sit down next to me. Now, from the minute I sat down I was totally focused on Bawa. I didn't even see who this was who was sitting next to me. So I snuck a look and thought, "She's pretty." Then Bawa gave us this blessing that this was a good marriage and he recommended it to Anne and myself. And he said that we would have similar destinies.

So then Anne and I took a walk and introduced ourselves since we really didn't know each other. We had seen each other around, but had never really spoken. We had a lot of similarities and we decided to go ahead and do as Bawa had recommended. We spent 20 years together in relative harmony, and went on to have a child, Kabira. She has turned out to be a powerful and loving person in her own right.

"Who is playing this part anyway? That's right, play it any way you want. That's the way to play it."

"This movie we're in is unpredictable at any time."

"This is a never-ending story we're involved in. We're just part of the acting crew."

"You always have to be prepared that the thing you want most desperately to happen may not happen the way you think, or it may never happen. That takes faith. So why not try wanting to see something happen without the desperation."

"The unexpected things in life are often the most interesting and can impact us greatly."

Original Stories

I left my position as Psychologist at Fort Dix in October 1974 and went to Ceylon, now called Sri Lanka, with my wife at the time. While I was there, I met several of Bawa's original disciples. One of them was named Father Tampo. He told me that when he was 15, he came down with a severe illness and went into a coma. He was in that coma for a number of years. He saw Bawa while he was in the coma. Then when he came out of the coma later on, he actually met Bawa. So Bawa came to him while he was in the coma indicating that he would see him again. Father Tampa was a real character. He had one tooth, walked around with no shoes, and had enormous feet. He had been some type of minister but had been ejected from the community at some point. He was an amazing character. He had absolutely no relatives and was totally alone in the world. He just laughed a lot.

On another occasion in late 1974, I walked along the seaside with one of Bawa's oldest disciples. He told me that several years before, one of Bawa's disciples who worked on a farm told Bawa that there were people there who were going to kill the disciple. Bawa said that he'd take care of it. This was told to Bawa while he was living at the Ashram in Jaffna in Ceylon. Now Bawa went to the farm and stayed there a month, foiling the attempt on this disciple's life. All the time Bawa was at the farm, he never left the Ashram in Jaffna. That's the total mystery of how Bawa could be.

"Sometimes it seems that the world is a very, very, large, insane asylum. We need only not get caught in others' madness and stick to our own."

"Intention to pray is even more powerful than physical prayer– but it's good to do both."

"We're here to open ourselves up. It's God's business to give everybody what they need on this journey to open them up."

"Don't overplay your part, underplay it. That's the way to play it effectively."

"There is no time– everything is going on right now at the same time. That's a total mind-blower."

Things Are Never What They Seem

In October 1974, a group of us went to Ceylon to be with the Guru. I was with Anne, my wife at the time. Up to that point, I actually don't remember having ever seen Bawa eat anything, and there was a general feeling amongst some of the people, including myself, that he didn't eat any food.

One day in Ceylon we went on a trip with Bawa. There were four other people in the car, with Bawa sitting in front. This was always a big deal to ride around the countryside with Bawa. Now we were on the road to visit his farm, which was quite a long way from the Ashram in Jaffra. So I was sitting in the back of the Morris Minor automobile and all of a sudden Bawa turns around to everybody, as if we were a bunch of guys riding around, and asks if we would like food. We all responded yes.

So we pulled around to a vendor who was selling roti's, which are a round biscuit. There were five of us in the car and the guru orders five biscuits from the vendor. Bawa hands a biscuit to each of the other people. There was one remaining, and he starts eating it. Now this may not seem like a big deal to people reading this, but to me it totally broke the idea that this being did not eat food. This experience actually brought me closer to him. Bawa used food a great deal in his teachings.

"How do we play our part, anyway? Play it any way you want– that's the way to play it."

"This movie we're in is unpredictable at every turn, and time is not what you think."

"There is no time. It's all one moment in time."

"There really is nothing to look forward to– just be you– it's good enough."

"Nothing in the future is going to make you happy. Be happy now."

Unexpected Guests

On another day in 1974 in Jaffna, in Ceylon, we again took a trip with the Guru to a place called Mankumban. We were engaged in helping to build what Bawa called, 'God's House,' on this sort of peninsula which was right on the Indian Ocean. We all traveled there and were engaged in building the house.

Sometimes Bawa would cook for everybody and on this particular day he asked everyone to have lunch, which he prepared in a huge cauldron over a wood fire. We would all gather banana leaves and come up to him, and he would spoon the food out onto the banana leaf for us to eat it. There were no utensils; we would use our fingers. This is the traditional Ceylonese style of eating. I watched Bawa as he was feeding one person at a time, and I was watching the food in the cauldron which was going down significantly to a lower level.

All of a sudden, a number of cars started arriving with the people from the town. They had known Bawa, and he invited them to have some food. As they started to line up to receive it, I looked at the amount of food in the cauldron and looked at the amount of people lining up. Given the proportions he was serving everyone, it seemed there was no way that he could feed them all, but he did. I was there and I witnessed this. I will never forget it.

"Learn to have mild disinterest in things– all things– a gentle dose of not caring."

"See if you can make yourself laugh– that's a good exercise."

"It's amazing how fast or slow a scene can change."

"People like to have alot of their stuff around– it reminds them of who they think they are. Isn't that amazing."

"It's amazing how you remember stuff– really."

Looking for Friends

In 1975, I had been with Bawa for about two years. Then one day, I read in one of Bawa's old discourses that he had said that the reason he had come to America was to find other people like himself. He indicated that he was a crazy man looking for others who had the same kind of craziness. So to me, that made sense because I had the same craziness.

Dying is simply showing up for your time of departure–from this realm.

There really is only one question– what is going on here? And there really is only one answer– whatever is up for you right now.

Why worry about anyone or anything– in fact, why worry at all?

Insanity is refusal to stay in the present as other people experience it. You see, insanity is really like getting caught in a time warp. You can't find your way out. So at some point, some people make a decision that they'd rather be with the insanity as others have defined it, and play in the game that most other people have accepted as reality.

Sometimes just sit down, have a cup of coffee with yourself. That can be a cool experience– of hanging out with yourself.

How the Guru Did It

Sometimes Bawa would seem dismissive, but he really knew why everybody came and what they came for. If people came to build up their own arrogance, he would give them what they needed at that time, which most often was not what they expected.

During 1976, the famous author Robert Bly was at the height of his career. He had written books for men primarily to get them in touch with their masculinity. He had become fairly well known, and had given performances in which he would speak and play on a ukulele. He was a real performer. Bawa asked him if he had a question, and Bly responded to Bawa, "Yes, what should I do?" Bawa said, "You have to stop talking, you talk too much." Bawa was telling this to a man who made his living as someone who spoke and performed.

Evidently, Bawa saw that at this period in Bly's life, he had to be silent. Now whether Bly took this advice or not, I don't know, but I was impressed that Bawa would be that straightforward with him.

So it was always a question of what you wanted. If you asked Bawa a question, you had to be ready to receive the answer. If you were ready, then you got the gift of how he saw things. You had a choice– to go with the way you saw things, or go with the way he saw things.

The important thing to remember is that we have a choice and continue to do so.

"Sometimes you think, "Is that going to really happen?" The thing you just thought about– it's really two different thoughts vying for your attention."

"You know it's good to have a friend who you can tell anything to– absolutely anything."

"Meher Baba said– Don't Worry, Be Happy– the only problem with that is you have to already be happy in order not to worry. Hmmmmmmmm. How does that work? Well, I guess there really is only one thing– Be Happy."

"Listen, you're not doing God any favors by praying. You're doing yourself a favor."

"Just be careful that your determination doesn't turn into your fanaticism."

The Mystery of Prayer

During the early 1980's, the Guru strongly urged us that it was good to do the Five Times Prayer in the way he had taught it to us. I fell right into line and did it. After awhile I noticed that hardly anyone else was doing it, and I began to question if I should continue doing it. Shortly after his request, the Guru was extremely ill. He had not left his room in two months. He was under continuous care.

One afternoon, I decided to go up into the Mosque which had been built onto the Guru's house. No one was around. In my heart I said to the Guru, "I need to see a sign that I should continue doing this prayer. If I don't see a sign by the time this prayer is over, I'm not doing it anymore." So I did the prayer and came down the steps, put on my coat, and said to the Guru on the inside, "That's it."

As I walked out the Mosque door, I looked to the right and the Guru was being wheeled around in a wheelchair completely bundled up with an oxygen tank attached to him. He did not even look at me as they wheeled him back up the stairs to his room. I knew then that I should continue doing that practice. I thought, "If he can get himself out of a sick bed after two months to go out into the cold to show me his presence, the least I can do is to do the prayers as he had directed us to do."

Since then, I have been fairly attached to this practice. So this practice of trusting Bawa is one of the first steps toward letting go. It becomes deeper and deeper and more and more of a mystery.

"If there's a vote taken as to which aspect of God I treasure the most, I'd say laughing."

"Are you thinking about tomorrow? There really is no tomorrow— not today. Everything exists within the right now and if there is a tomorrow, then that will be right now."

"Don't focus on the pain in the world. Focus on what will keep you sane in the world."

"Allow yourself, if only for a short moment, to go to that place where you cannot possibly think of one more thing that you need to do. Go there and see what happens."

"When you get to a point where there's absolutely nothing you can count on in this world, you're home free."

Attachments

One day we were in Bawa's room and a couple came in. They had had a child two years previously. It was their only child and they were somewhat older in life. They lived in a house which had a pool. Two weeks before, the child fell in the pool and drowned.

Now these two approached Bawa and they looked extremely unhappy and miserable. Bawa looked at them for a long time and said, "You being so unhappy and miserable shows me that you do not understand what really happened. That child came into the world to just spend two years and it completed its work. All of your unhappiness is due to your attachment. You must let go of that attachment. That is what is making you miserable. I was present during this talk, and this story later had a profound effect on me in terms of how I saw death.

"Basically each one of us is alone here. Everything else is show biz."

"Sometimes things just don't make sense and sometimes, they make even less sense."

"Sometimes things seem out of our hands. They are, mostly. The great paradox is that this thing is totally out of our hands, or are we creating this as we go along? Then the issue is– who is the Creator?"

"Things are never really falling apart– they're just sort of getting rearranged."

"Some people are afraid of being alone– really alone. We need this experience in order to realize that we really are totally alone. How could that be, since we have all these characters within us? Look at all those characters we're carrying around within us– an actual traveling circus."

Sai Baba

You could never tell what Bawa was going to do. It was related to me that when Bawa was in his room in Philadelphia in 1984, someone came to see him. He presented himself as a very spiritual person to Bawa and that he had been with Sai Baba and that he in fact was one of Sai Baba's closest people. Sai Baba was, at that time, becoming known as an individual who could manifest objects out of the air. Bawa said that was no big deal, that the man was merely a magician.

This man who presented himself in front of Bawa indicated that he was so close to Sai Baba, that Sai Baba let him drink some of his special elixir that would produce great powers. It was actually a kind of sandy substance. This man had a vial of that substance to show Bawa and presented it to Bawa as if it were a kind of holy relic. Bawa raised it to the light and took a long look. He then proceeded to empty the contents of the vial into the trash bin. Bawa told the man, "Why are you taking this stuff," and then proceeded to tell him that the vial contained many discarded articles such as dried menstrual tissue, rat guts, parts of bones and various incantations.

In essence, Bawa was telling this person, "This is how a magician operates," referring to Sai Baba. I don't think we saw that fellow again.

"We have to be rid of all paradigms, I mean all, and go to that place where all paradigms dissolve. That's what this certainly is all about; especially the scary paradigms. Do you really think that we are all going to Hell, or even Heaven? This is not about punishment and reward. We already have the reward. It's the grace of this journey into the heart of the Creator and being a part of that creation."

"Patience blocks fear."

"Everyone has their own drama. If you want to join the others, go ahead if you want to do that. Or, you can stick to your own. Sometimes it's a lot easier that way."

"If we want less and less, we may in fact receive more and more of what we need. It may work like that."

"Tell yourself a story— go ahead— any story. It doesn't have to be true. Maybe it's something you want to see happen, or something that has already happened. It's just a story."

Guru as Student

Bawa was a total mystery, because many of us thought that he was beyond an emotional response to the activities of the world, and that he was in that state where he could just observe and not be affected. This was also my thinking.

In 1984, Mitch Gilbert died. He was one person who Bawa had always trusted to speak on his behalf. Mitch would often give a little talk right before Bawa would give his discourse. When Mitchell died relatively suddenly, it seemed to me, as I watched Bawa, that he was emotionally affected by the death of the one person who he seemed to trust the most when it came to his teaching. This is a significant part of the Guru's teaching for me, because I wanted Bawa to be perfect.

Bawa, himself, said that he was not a Guru and was in fact a student learning from us. This is profound because we want to be in the presence of the perfected being. To this day, many of the followers of Bawa still find it hard to accept that he was a student. The fact that Bawa was still learning put him on another level for me. I saw him as being much more human, much more real, much more in the process and having not completed the process.

"How does it all work? I have no idea. It may have something to do with trusting the process of your life totally."

"I don't think that the Creator cares about what we think. It's the actions that count."

"Comforting others can be tricky. It can get real sticky, if we think we are the comforter. There really is only one comforter."

"It's when we limit our choices that we actually begin to hone in on what we really want to do. This gives us direction– but what if we choose to do something that doesn't turn out the way we thought we were directed? Then we deal with that until the next choice. In a sense, every day we get to redefine ourselves. Of course, that definition gets to be redefined in its time. And that's how we keep evolving."

"It's not our job to pick up another's fears or even their strengths. Work on your own fears and strengths, that's your spiritual practice."

The Building of the Mosque

On a particular day in 1984, Bawa let us know that we were going to build a Mosque. There was a good deal of opposition to that. Many people came to Bawa to get away from religion. Bawa had said, "This is not about religion, this is about unity. Whatever we do with this Mosque is to give people the experience of unity." So I wondered what, if anything, was my role? Did I have a part to play in this?

Just as the foundation of the Mosque was starting to be laid, I had a dream. In the dream, I left my house in Havertown, PA, and as I left, my house caught on fire. So I started to wander around and I came to a huge magnificent garden that had a thick, heavenly scent. A rider was coming towards me on a horse. He was wearing a cape and a military type hat that resembled that of the old times and he held a sword. As this rider came up to me, I realized I knew who he was. It was Chuck, one of the Fellowship people and a friend of mine who was supervising the building of the Mosque. I said to him, "Chuck, I'm lost. I can't find my way back home." He said, "That's alright, I need a Mosque worker." And the dream ended.

The next day I went to the work site and somebody handed me a belt full of tools to help with the building. I labored daily for eight to ten hours for the next three months. An unusual work energy came to me to help build the Mosque. It seemed to me that the energy that I was experiencing was way beyond my normal abilities. I always remembered the dream that led me to do that work. Things were like that around Bawa. You had to be ready to play whatever role seemed to be indicated. This was yet another exercise in letting go and letting things evolve.

We don't always know what the next thing will bring, but if we're open to it and it seems to lead in a direction which is correct, then we have to go with it and see what happens. Bawa said that when the call to prayer is given in this Mosque, it reaches 70,000 miles into the sky. Sometimes now, when I get to give the call to prayer, I think about that.

"Maybe, just maybe, when this is all over and we meet on the other side, we'll just compare notes on how we did and have a big laugh."

"No one knows who anyone else really is. We're just getting the outside version. It's all about love, anyway."

"Things can change fast if we are alert, or things can change slowly if we are even more alert."

"Where do the scenes come from, since space and time do not really exist? They come from somewhere, and where is that? Well, that's the point of the mystery … to experience where somewhere is. I believe it has something to do with quiet and having no expectations."

Mystical Experience

The Mosque opened in Philadelphia, as part of the Bawa Muhaiyaddeen Fellowship. Not everybody was happy with that decision. Some people said, "Why are we going to do these kinds of prayers?" Bawa answered, "When you do these prayers, it's not like religion. For my children it means something else." So right from the beginning, the Mosque turned out to be a kind of mystical place for me, especially the first three days after the mosque was built.

One day we were lined up for the morning prayer, called Fajr. In those days, we all wore our white jibbas which were a kind of cassack. We are all lined up and I see someone standing in front of the line facing us, also dressed in white. He's walking down the line sort of taking notes of who's there. Then he disappears and prayers continue. That evening, I told Bawa the story. Bawa said, "Right, that's how it is. Every time you pray, it's being recorded." I keep looking for that man again, dressed in white taking the roll, but I've never seen him since.

After a few days of the Mosque being built and prayers being established, the attendance of the prayers diminished significantly. This especially happened during the morning prayers. Someone mentioned that to Bawa, and he said, "You think this Mosque is just for

you? This mosque is full of people, praying all the time."
A couple of days later, I walked up to the Mosque. There
wasn't anybody else there, but I saw a place full of people
dressed in white praying; then they all disappeared. I
told this to Bawa and he again said, "Yes, this is the way
that it is."

*"Each one of us is made up of many different people. Who
we want to be at any one time is up to us, no one else. We
don't always have to play the same part."*

**"Sometimes the best way to really love someone is to
leave them alone."**

*"Who made up all these rules anyway? If you think God's
got rules, then you need another view of God."*

*"Things may make sense at the time we do them. Then
later on, they may make absolutely no sense at all. Isn't
that amazing? Actually often they don't make any sense
even while we're doing them."*

**"The more we cling to the known, the more fearful
we are of the unknown."**

*"The less you think you know, the more will be known. It's
amazing what you can know when you let go of being the
knower."*

Happenings in the Mosque

Sometimes things happened in the Mosque that seemed like a psychotic hallucination, but they actually occurred. Now these experiences I'm sharing were entirely my own. They were not group experiences and no one else could verify any of these.

Soon after the Mosque was built, I was sitting there and I started to think that I was really getting hungry. I thought that I just might leave. At that very moment, a loaf of bread dropped into my lap. Then it disappeared and I was no longer hungry. That actually is one of the most amazing experiences I've ever had, because it was almost as though I could feel the bread.

On another occasion, a group of us were singing the end of a prayer going to a fairly high pitch. I looked up and the roof was off of the Mosque and the sky was showing. There was a golden chain that came down, and the person leading the prayers was at the end of the chain. Then the roof was there again, and that scene was over. I posed that story to Bawa, and he replied, "Yes it's like that. This is a very powerful part of the universe right now."

"Patience slows down time and more can happen when time is slowed down. That's the secret of patience."

"Why wouldn't there be divine humor. That's what the religious sometimes forget."

"Once you individuate from the Guru, you're on your own Guru journey."

"For a man, he has to learn how to get along without a woman for periods of time. For a woman, she has to learn how to get along without a man for periods of time. That's how men and women learn to be able to get along with each other."

"Every day, each day is the most important day of your life."

Mosque Experience

I recall an experience in which I saw beings of light in the Mosque. When I looked at these beings I got this enormous sense that they were presenting a serene patience. I told this to Bawa and he said that it was the prophet and his companions.

Now these are amazing experiences which I don't pretend to understand totally. For example, some questions I have asked are, "Where did these experiences come from?" and, "Do they exist even now as I write this?" It's an amazing mystery.

"When you are around people who are really suffering, you get to experience some of their suffering and that can make you stronger in your faith."

"God gives you an infinite amount of time."

"To pray with others is good. To pray alone is even better."

"There's always less to do than you think. If there's more to do than you think, then do that also."

"I mean when you really, really, really think about it, the whole trip is really, really unbelievable."

So You Want a Perfect Guru?

Two days after my arrival home from Mecca in 1985, I had an accident. I had a pool in the backyard of my house at that time and was cleaning out the pool. All of a sudden, I found myself falling into the pool. It was only four feet deep but the way I landed fractured my ankle. It was a total freak accident. I couldn't figure that one out, even to this day. It was almost as if I was propelled into the pool.

Anyway, after a few days of hobbling around on crutches I managed to get myself over to see Bawa. This accident was a great mystery to me and I wondered why it had happened. I arrived to Bawa's room and he was sitting on his bed. He looked at me and asked me what happened. After I told him, he had the most perplexed look on his face. I had expected that he would know why this happened. As far as I could determine, Bawa, himself, did not know. This, in a sense, altered my relationship to Bawa into a more mature state. I had assumed up to that time that he knew everything. I then realized that he also experienced life as a total mystery. That really connected me to him.

"There are no coming attractions. It's all here right now. The whole thing is being created right now."

"You know, sometimes there's absolutely nothing you can say about what you've been through, nothing. The whole trip is mind boggling. All you can do is to shake your head and smile."

"Patience is always indicated– especially if you're in a hurry."

"Love is strange. It comes in different forms. All of them are from the same root, and that's how your love grows— from that root."

"Patience is good. It lengthens the scene so you can see what needs to be seen."

Going to Mecca

In 1985, I had a sort of mystical dream about going to Mecca. I took the dream to the Guru and he said, "Yes, that would be good." He indicated that I would be representing him there along with three other people. This was a great mystery to me because I had never expected to do this. I never wanted to be in huge crowds of people; I didn't even want to be identified as a Muslim. The Guru gave me an Arabic name. My Arabic name is Muhammad Razzaq, which means 'The Provider' in Arabic. I thought, "That's a pretty good name." So we went to Mecca and it was amazing. There were probably two million people there– all Muslims– praying at the same time. Unbelievable.

Something very special took place for me in Mecca in 1985. When I reached Mecca, the experience was so powerful, that I actually did not have a single thought for the next three days. Then on the fourth day, after taking some rest one morning, I experienced seeing myself looking at my image from another dimension. It was definitely me; it wasn't a drawing, or painting, or picture. It was me, alive, observing and smiling. It actually felt like that transcended aspect of myself which totally confirmed my existence. It was an amazing event to me.

When I returned to Philadelphia I told this story

to the Guru. He said, "Yes, that's correct, and the ones around you who are observing you are the prophet and his companions." This is an experience which I had in no way planned, and resulted because I was in a total state of no thoughts and no expectations. I believe we can all have this at some point in our lives. It may not have to take such a profound change in environment to bring it on, but that level of reality to me does exist.

"Religion will not get us where we need to go. It just goes so far, and then we're on our own toward the open space where there are no religious practices or beliefs."

"Laughing out loud is good. Laughing inside is even better. Silence on the outside is good, silence on the inside is even better. Prayer on the outside is good, prayer on the inside is even better."

"What's the point of keeping all your love inside? It'll get stale if you don't use it."

"Do everything as if it's the last thing you're ever going to do– and then just let go."

"Sometimes instead of creating a scene it's better to quietly slip out of the scene, practically unseen. It saves a lot of drama, unless of course you're into more drama in your life, in which case, go ahead and make a scene and see what happens."

Individuation

Upon our return from Mecca to Philadelphia in 1985, the four of us were called into the Guru's room to welcome us back. So he's giving high praises to the three other people. Then he turns to me and says, "You have to go back. All you did was to look at the women, looking at their ankles." Bawa said this to me, but in reality all the women are all wrapped up in various layers of garments. There is really no one to look at in that way there.

Everybody was crowded around us in the room as the Guru was speaking. So now the Guru was saying, in essence, that I failed. As this was going on, I began to feel more and more on my own because I knew what he was saying really had nothing to do with me, in the sense that it was not my reality. I felt a sense of uniqueness from the rest of the group and the Guru because, as this was playing out, it was a kind of secret between the Guru and myself.

So, on the one hand I was being presented with a reality from the Guru, which was totally separate from my own. It was a great learning for me and I then realized that an even deeper, true relationship with the Guru is on the inside. It remains a continuing mystery.

"Picture yourself sitting in the middle of a junkyard, and there is light all around you. That's a good one."

"You have to admit that this is a very strange life. If you don't admit it, then you have a very high threshold for strangeness, and more power to you."

"Just tell yourself you're good. That'll take care of any idea that you have about not being good enough."

"You know when you really, really think about it, the whole digital reality is a real trip. The left side of the brain is for figuring– the right side is for doing."

"Did you ever do something and right after, you think, "Did that really happen?" Or you can't even remember what happened. Hmmmmmmm."

Precognition

In 1985, I had a Psychology practice at the Center for Preventive Medicine in Bala Cynwyd, PA. My practice was falling off and I had decided to get a regular job. I was accepted as a Psychologist at a facility which dealt with nuns and priests who were sexual abusers; the only facility of its kind in the country at the time. I was going to accept the position the next day.

That evening I had an experience as I was sleeping. In a vision, I was in my office at the Center for Preventive Medicine. I heard a number of patients coming up the steps; there was a large crowd. They all plowed into my very small waiting room, along with the Guru. Everyone was sitting around him. I heard them and was about to go into the waiting room to join them. The Guru said, "No, you stay in your doctor's office." I looked around the room. Everybody there was someone I knew. When I awoke in the morning, I knew that I was not to take the position.

During the next two years, everyone in that room came to see me as a patient. That's the kind of relationship we have with the inner Guru.

"You know you can be as sweet as you want, or as tough as you want, or both at the same time."

"Just assume that you don't know anything— that's a good place to start from in any situation."

"Love is the antidote for all the fears, questions and worries that we accumulate in life."

"Isn't it amazing how you can actually remember things? Where are they when you're not remembering them?"

"Religions are strange. They seem to be caught in some dream which they won't give up and trying to convince others of the truth of their dream, when in fact each person is having their own dream. Take what you need from the religions, leave the rest, and be all right with that."

A Lesson in Detachment

In the early 90's, my family and I were on a vacation in Canada. At that time my daughter, Kabira was 12 years old. One evening, while we were there, I had this intense dream which lasted all night. I dreamt that my daughter died, and I spent the entire night of the dream going around and telling people we knew that she had died. When I woke up in the morning, I had this enormous sense of relief. I had a feeling that in some way my attachment to my daughter had been lifted from me. It's not that I didn't continue to love her, but somehow I felt less enmeshed with her life process.

"Once you set out for something, there may be obstacles. Avoid that which you feel safe to avoid, and approach that which you feel safe to approach. That's how we go through the obstacles."

"In a sense we have to keep sweeping out the trash. It all has to go. Your whole history– it has to go. The whole trip has to go so that you can go on."

"You know there are a lot of different aspects to ourselves. It's good to meet them, even engage them if we want to, or just say, "The hell with them.""

"How do you not let things bother you? By placing yourself out of the physical and emotional range of that which is bothering you."

"When you say, "I'm just gonna think about God," what are you thinking about?"

Different Prescriptions

The big issue about people coming from all around asking, "What should I do?" is that the response that Bawa would give to one person may not have applied to you if you were also sitting there. Some people thought Bawa was making a rule or some pronouncement. Well, he may have been doing that for that particular person, but it may not have applied to you at that same time. That's how people got upset or confused because they would not discriminate between what Bawa was saying to one person and what he was saying to them, but on an inside level. This is the general danger of groups. People might have come because they want to individuate, but actually they would coagulate.

The real teacher will help you with that process of discrimination. Sometimes people would remark to Bawa, saying, "But you said the opposite thing last week to that other person." Bawa would then say, "That was then, this is now." So the process of unearthing the wisdom within us is just this– to discriminate between what refers to us or has nothing to do with us.

"So how do we do this trip, knowing it's all an illusion? How do we do that? We can't do that. We can only hang on for the ride."

"You know there's plenty of love to go around. It takes the right situation to bring it out of people– and all situations are right."

"Sometimes it seems that we initiate a scene and sometimes it seems that we're just taking part in the scene. Actually, we're initiating them all."

"If you plan on becoming sick then guess what– you may get sick. If you don't plan on being sick you might get sick but you won't feel victimized."

"It's hard to believe that the truth lies within us. What about the churches, temples, mosques, bibles and scriptures? They may offer comfort. If they cause you discomfort, toss them."

We Always Have Choices

Sometimes Bawa would give people choices. A friend of mine was pregnant and came to see Bawa at about the sixth or seventh month. During that time, Bawa spoke to the mother and said, "This is going to be a very difficult pregnancy. You can go through with this if you choose, with all the difficulties that it will entail, or you can choose to have that child be taken back." She chose to go ahead and went through some difficult times. The child was two months premature and was on life support for several weeks.

That was about thirty years ago. Today that child is in medical school. Bawa always gave us the element of choice.

"Contentment? Hmmmmmmmmm. That's a really deep one. It requires diving deep into the moment and bringing up that contentment which lies deep within us. You may want to put your life behind you so that it doesn't impede your way deeper. It's all right to do something really slowly if that's what it takes to do the thing you want to do."

"The world attracts and distracts at the same time. Make sure you know the difference and go with that in mind."

"You never know what you can handle until it comes time to handle it. The less you think about it the better you'll handle it."

"It's almost as important to know what you need to not do, as what you need to do. Actually it may be more important, since it may save you a great deal of effort and possible aggravation. This is where restraint comes in handy."

"It's not the job of the child to make the parent happy. It's the job of the parent to take care of their own happiness."

Great Teaching

When Bawa played a scene, he was not in the same time dimension as others. He was in his own time dimension, as we all are. Now sometimes we would be sitting around his room and he would just sit there quietly. But there was always an anticipatory aspect to it … that something was going to happen. And sure enough, a person would arrive and sit down in the room as part of the circle surrounding Bawa's bed, and as soon as that person would sit down, he would start whatever he had to say or do.

Now the room might have 50 or 60 people in it and as he spoke he got stronger and stronger and he would sweep the room, taking everybody in. As he was making various points he would sometimes make a point and look at me straight in the eyes, and say, "I'm talking to you," and continue on with his points.

So at the end of the meeting, I would say to some of my friends who were there, "Did you see how Bawa looked at me at that time? It was amazing!" Nevertheless, none of them would have seen it. It showed me that Bawa was in another time dimension and could more or less split the time of interaction with a person so that only he and the person knew it was happening at that time.

Now I'm not saying he did this consciously or as a

skill, but I'm saying that he was in that dimension. He spoke from that dimension. Otherwise, to tell the truth, I don't think many of us would have stayed around day after day and year after year. He was teaching us how to access that part of ourselves which was beyond ordinary time and space by actually taking us into that dimension.

"If you let your heart rule you, you'll have a good ruler by which to measure things. This can be called wisdom."

"Everyone really is an independent person. When we become a dependent person, we lose our independence. A good part of our work is to reclaim that independent person by letting go of our need for dependence. Dependence enslaves us."

"Obsessing about things isn't good for you. It's a form of possessing things, and at some level of awareness, we possess nothing. That's how we get free of being possessed by our possessions."

"Once we step out of the picture which we have made ourselves part of, if only temporarily, our life changes."

"If you take care of the small things with ease, then there are no big things to take care of. This is how we reduce our drama."

Meeting with the Prophets

It was impossible to tell whether Bawa actually slept or not. He appeared to be sleeping and all of a sudden he would jolt up in his bed and say, "I just had a meeting with some of the prophets. Then he would tell us what the prophets said. He actually seemed to be able to converse with the prophets.

One day I was in the Mosque. A part of the prayers in the morning that we had done and continued to do was to give our greetings to the eight major prophets as Bawa had instructed. These prophets are Adam, Noah, Abraham, Ishmael, Moses, David, Jesus, and Mohammed. Now we would repeat these names every morning. So one morning, throughout the prayers that we were doing, I kept thinking, "Where are the prophets?" I continued to think about this from the beginning to the end, which took an hour. Then we finally came to say the prophet's names, beginning with Adam. Each time we said one of the prophet's names I felt a kiss on my forehead. Now this happened eight times in a row. I genuinely felt that I had been visited by the prophets.

"There is no end to the story. Isn't it amazing that something is really, really important one moment, and then minutes later it has lost all importance? What happened? It seems like it's gone away; it's been diffused. Amazing."

"If you feel trapped in a situation and are complaining about it, figure out how to untrap yourself and stop complaining. Save your energy for further figuring out and when there is an increase in courage."

"In a sense, all life is a prank. We are not who we appear to be and no one else is as they appear to be. So how can we handle that little mystery? This whole business about God – what's that all about? No one knows anything about that either. We really are on our own here to try and figure it out."

"Men and women can be an attraction or a distraction for each other. Make your choice."

"It may be good to break a pattern if that pattern is starting to feel too restraining. Then it may need a little loosening of the restraints."

The Divine Assembly

The Guru said the most extraordinary things to us. He said there was a divine assembly that ruled the universe. He also said that he came from that divine assembly and that he was the head of that divine assembly. His job was to bring people back with him; one out of 100,000,000 people could do this.

He said that he had already brought eight-and-a-half people over– we wondered who the half person was.

So for me, that continues to be a mystery. I cannot even begin to wrap my head around this one. But I accept the possibility that this might in fact be true.

"God is continuously learning from his creations. We think God knows what's going to happen next? Hmmmmmm … I wonder."

"To help a friend is really good. To help yourself is also really good. To help a stranger is the very best."

"There are many ways to scare people. Religion seems to be the best of these."

"If you can remain with absolutely nothing to do for even a short period of time– that's a taste of freedom. Being busy is ok, not being busy is also ok. Not caring whether you're busy or not busy is really ok."

"We have arrived here in this illusory place. Now we just have to figure out how to deal with this grand illusion of our life."

Continuing Education

Bawa opened up the picture of reality to us and indicated that there was always more to be learned. Even after 40 years I can say for myself that it's still happening. Whatever that process was, it's still happening. What I mean to say is that this is the secret and the mystery of the inner Guru.

The secret is that we have to keep learning and experiencing our reality, or what appears to be our reality. Nothing is fixed – everything is in the process of evolving.

"If something isn't working for you, then something else is working for you. Every situation is repairable if we choose not to be impaired or despaired."

"Don't take everything so seriously, especially yourself. It isn't what you think, anyway."

"If we're looking for peace from the world, forget it. We have to find our own inside. It's actually easier to find."

"Give any idea time to sink in. If it sinks let it go. If it rises to the surface, go with it."

"Most people talk too much about the past. Let the past pass into the past."

Guru as Mirror

Bawa had different ways of treating different illnesses and you never knew what he was going to prescribe. Sometimes I would bring a patient to Bawa and there were some occasions in which they were quite ill.

One time, I brought someone to Bawa. I forget the exact ailment, but Bawa surprised everyone by prescribing the blood of young pigeons. He asked the person to tame these pigeons and then drain their blood after they were killed, and rub that over those parts of their body that had the problem. That was such an outrageous prescription to me; it became obvious to me that he was seeing something about the person and the illness that enabled him to prescribe that particular remedy.

It was really going on all the time, because sometimes he would say, "Everything that I do is for a purpose. If I touch you in a certain way or look at you in a certain way– that has a purpose." The whole experience about Bawa, which continues to be, is the issue of surrender, and is one in which you lose yourself and go to a higher aspect of yourself.

But then you begin to realize that there is no difference between you and the Guru and you have to take off and become the Guru. That's scary, because, in essence, your experience of the Guru is actually the experience of yourself. The Guru is the mirror. That's why you really

68

can't, in many respects, worship the guru because you're worshipping a projection of yourself.

"Don't take pride to prayer. Take prayer to pride and eliminate it. It's not a good friend, actually."

"Improve on the Guru. Don't get stuck on the Guru."

"If you have to separate yourself from things, or someone else, do it without a big attitude."

"Everything that's happened to you up to this point in your life is all nostalgia of equal intensity. We're the ones who imbue the nostalgia with emotion."

"If you want to be a radical theologian, you have to be able to say, "I have no idea what is going on." That's being a radical theologian."

The Highest Teaching

Now very often we would sit around Bawa's bed when he was in Philadelphia and maybe just a handful of people of 30 or so would be in and out of his room. If you didn't have a lot of things to do that day, you could hang around with the Guru. There may not have been that much happening, and in fact it may have gone on for seven or eight hours that way. Then after thinking, "Well, I'm just gonna leave," Bawa would say, "It's all a lie. It's all an illusion. It's all a dream. It's all gone. It's all right. Let's see what happens next."

So for me, those words were actually the most profound things that he has ever said and continue to be so for me. It sums up his teaching. The experience of being with Bawa was like an ancient experience—an original experience when things were new and the whole story started. So the key, I think for all of us, is to be able to live in multiple realities and allow them to merge within us as one reality.

*"**The best way to do something is to do it without thought. That's real concentration.**"*

"The world is a university."

"If you're discouraged, then be discouraged. See how far that takes you. Then try encouragement. It'll probably take you a bit farther into your courage."

"Do whatever you have to do that's right in front you. Let everything else go. That's concentration."

"Sometimes you realize that everything you do is amazing, if you really think about it."

The Value of Prayer

Bawa said, "This is not a religion we're doing here," because when he decided to build the Mosque, people came to complain. They said, "We didn't come here to do religion, we all came from religions. We're trying to get out of religions." He would respond, "When my children pray here, it is not religion." So even if you're doing the Five Times Prayer, if you choose to do that, you're not doing it as religion. He said these practices are good for your health, especially early-morning prayer. He said it was very good to be up at four in the morning because that's when there is the most clarity.

"Satan is that part of us which does not believe that we are totally connected to the source and creator of all wisdom and love."

"You have to surrender everything because you don't know how it's going to turn out. That's what makes it all so mysterious."

"Do not remain loyal to those or that which is disloyal to you. Loyalty is not always a human obligation."

"Sometimes you may feel "I don't fit in here." Good."

"Keep your life as simple as possible. That leaves room for the impossible to become possible."

Handling the World

One day, Bawa said, "We need to be like a thief in the world." You had to not get caught by anything in the world that was trying to get ahold of you, and you did that by being a thief. When I heard that, I felt that it was a very powerful image for me, and that it is true.

It is true because, in a sense, we have to allow ourselves to be present in the scenes and yet be an observer of the scene. So, the thief part relates to taking back from the world the part that is attracting us.

"Breaking paradigms is scary. Not breaking them is even scarier. Life is scary, but mostly we scare ourselves."

"When you treat every scene as a sacred scene, your life will become sacred."

"Religions can be lethal. If they are for you, there is an antidote. It's called faith, which has nothing to do with religion. What's the point of having faith in religion? Better to have faith in the Creator of all faith."

"Why do we think God is watching us? Maybe God is the one doing the whole trip."

"Every once in awhile, have a really good argument with yourself. I mean really get angry. Take both sides. Then look in the mirror, and just have a good laugh."

Taking the Guru's Advice

Periodically I would tell Bawa that I wanted to quit the field of Psychology. He'd say, "No, stay with it. You're trained to do that." So then one day I announced to him that I was definitely quitting Psychology. He said, "No, no you stay with it." He said, "What I'm going to do is I will help you with Psychology. When anyone comes to see you, you hand them over to me and then they will be seeing me, not you." He said, "The way we're going to do this is I'm going to teach you two things; the first is to drain the Schuylkill River and the second thing is I'm going to teach you how to shave a donkey." This was a kind of koan that he left me with, but the main point was that he would in fact handle the patients.

So now whenever I enter into that kind of situation where I am asked to play the role of Psychologist, I remember that I'm not the one doing this. It helps me to stay out of the state of the doer and allow whatever needs to unfold to happen.

"You know when you're by yourself you can say the most outrageous things. No one is listening."

"When you're in the role of the teacher, the teacher must take on the role of the student and learn from him or her."

"Worrying about tomorrow, today? Hmmmmmm. Why?"

"Babies are the latest dispatch from the Creator of everything."

"How do things get to be how they are? Why are things the way they are? That's the great mystery."

The Train Ride

The entire time I was in Ceylon with Bawa I was mostly thinking of how to get out of it. Of course I couldn't, because the set up was that I was going to learn a lot of things there. Anyway, I often had this mental image of 'getting out of there.'

So, one evening I had this dream vision while I was in Ceylon of being on a train. I was in one of the rear cars in the train, and had decided that I had to go and talk to the engineer, so I could stop the train to get off. I walked toward the front of the train and experienced some type of drama taking place in each car that I went through. I could see that I could get involved in the drama or keep moving forward. I get up to the engine room finally and open the door. The engineer was facing forward, dressed in a typical engineer's uniform. I say to the engineer, "You need to stop this train, I need to get off." The engineer turns his head toward me, shaking it, saying no. It is Bawa, smiling and indicating that this train is not stopping.

"Really, really there is no dying for us. Remember?"

"If you pray– don't ask for anything. Just pray. See what happens."

"If you do not fear rejection, then you are free to take risks."

"If you really love someone, be very careful– it's a very delicate instrument."

"You don't have to lead your life for others– just lead your life."

Passing On

The Fellowship has a burial ground which is one hour from the Mosque, southwest of Philadelphia. Part of the experience of being with Bawa was to learn the process of death. He felt that it was important that we have our own cemetary. At this point, there are about 150 people buried in the cemetary at the farm.

The whole arena of the farm and the burial grounds is a mystical place. Some people now buried at the farm are people who just came to the Fellowship for a short period of time and then left. Others are people who have been around for a long time, or who we had never met before.

It's an amazing experience to personally bury people that you know and to prepare their body, wash it down, wrap it in a shroud, personally place it in the grave, then fill the grave and say some prayers. It takes away all the previous learning that we have of burials and death. It's an amazing process when people that you know and love for a long time are beginning to pass away, one by one.

"Unless you admit it to yourself, that you don't know what is going on, will you experience what is going on. It's the ultimate paradox of life."

"Let's face it– Everyone has their own way to pray, or not to pray."

"Isn't it a trip– some people are paid religious leaders. What's that all about?"

"Your home should be your sanctuary. If it's not, it needs some rehab."

"We're making this movie up as we go along, and we don't know how it ends or even if it does end."

The Mazar

The Mazar where Bawa is buried continues to be an amazing place. People are coming from all over the country to visit– sometimes busloads of people. Somehow they're being drawn to the Mazar. Everyone seems to come for a different reason. Some people come because they see the Mazar as a shrine of a saint.

It is a tradition among the Sufis to visit a place where a very wise person is buried. They feel it as a boon to their life to visit a holy person. They also feel that they will receive many graces for this.

Bawa did say that the area around the Mazar would become a sacred place. It appears to be happening, and we never know who's going to show up.

"When you have nothing other than your breath, then you are fully alive."

"Any thought can pop into your head at any moment. Where do these thoughts come from?"

"No one's part in this play is more important than anyone else's. It's good to remember that."

"When you smell a flower, where is the smell before you smell the flower? Think about that one."

"Love everyone. Why not? Give it a try."

Eugene Ochs

Another amazing aspect of the Mazar is that the first person who was buried at the farm after Bawa passed, and the Mazar was built, was a man named Eugene Ochs. Eugene had come to the Fellowship a few years previously, and was the least likely character to visit Bawa then anyone could imagine. He appeared to come right out of the Kentucky Ozarks – he had that characteristic about him. He knew nothing about Sufism or any of the things that were being talked about by Bawa. He rarely spoke himself. No one really knew who he was.

Then one day he passed away and wound up being buried 20 feet from Bawa. This man who no one knew anything about, who appeared to be somewhat of an illiterate, is buried right there. So it's just part of this amazing mystery that surrounds Bawa Muhaiyaddeen.

So even now, sometimes someone will say, "Who was Eugene Ochs, anyway?"

"When you really merge with someone, it's not that you merge with them, you're merging with love."

"Sometimes you wonder, "How did I get myself into that mess? Why did I take that on?" You know, you couldn't really have done anything different at that time. Now maybe, if that comes around again, you might not do anything at all about it, and let it pass without a thought."

"No matter how you imagine something to be, it's not what you imagine it to be. Any thought you have isn't real or a big deal."

"Receiving love is great. Giving love is even greater."

"Everyone's story is just their story. It may have something to do with you, or nothing to do with you."

True Unity

There are lots of stories relating to the people who came to be with Bawa. No two people were alike, and everyone had a very singular relationship to Bawa. That also continues with new people who show up at the Fellowship. They also seem to have a very independent relationship to that little man who I listened to for over twelve years.

You see everything that happened with Bawa was a mystery. Nothing seemed to make sense, but somehow it appeared very real, and part of the story which we were involved in. This was almost like stepping into a storybook and becoming one of the characters. This was because Bawa, in essence, was the most amazing character of all, and by his very being, people had a more expansive experience of their own reality. That's why he often spoke about unity.

What he really meant for us was to learn to be in touch with all the aspects of our own self in a unified way. By doing that we would experience unity with others.

"There are no guarantees of how things are going to work out. They're actually working out the way they need to be working out, no matter how outrageous they seem."

"Life is a blank book. Write about what you want to see happen and then step back– and experience what you've written."

"The only thing we really have to give to people is our love."

"Stay out of situations that you don't absolutely have to get involved in."

"Be like a detective. See what's going on around you."

A Sufi Story

There's a Sufi story about King Solomon. One day one of his followers was walking down the street and he saw the Angel of Death. The Angel of Death actually had a surprised look on his face. The man took off and went to King Solomon. He said, "You have to get me out of here. I just saw the Angel of Death and I know he's after me." At first Solomon said, "I can't interfere with the work of the Angel of Death." Then Solomon said, "Where do you want to go to?" "Transport me to the Himalayan Mountains. He'll never find me there," the man said, and Solomon did so.

Then, the Angel of Death came to see Solomon. Solomon said, "Why are you going around scaring my people with a strange expression on your face?" The Angel said, "You're right, I was just very surprised this afternoon when I saw the man in town who I was supposed to take in the Himalayan Mountains this evening and I didn't know how that could happen."

"If something looks fishy it just might be— keep your eyes and ears open. This is called discriminative wisdom which is needed here in the world of illusion."

"The funny thing about prayers is you can absolutely make them up yourself— if you want to."

"Planning ahead is good— it sets direction."

"What happens when you run out of patience? Just exert a little bit more. Keep stretching it."

"Worry has everything to do with lack of faith, and lack of faith has a lot to do with not believing in yourself as much as you believe in others."

Singular Prescriptions

Bawa had different things to say to different people about health. It was important, when you were with him, to distinguish your own issues from other people's issues. This was because Bawa actually had a different prescription for each person. He never said the same thing to two different people. He also had no fixed formula for anything.

He tuned in to how the person related to their illness. Some people would come and he would prescribe chicken soup. Another person would come and he would prescribe meat. Another person would come and he would prescribe a total vegetarian diet. He would look at the person and I frequently watched him as he did this. He would look at the whole person and why that person had come. He would give them the history of the illness.

Of course, the main ingredients that he always emphasized were faith and determination. He said it was all right to have confidence in the prescription and that if he sent you to a doctor you would have confidence in the doctor. But he stressed that you remember the main focus was to first have confidence in God, who was really doing the treating.

"You don't own your life– it's on loan."

"We've come here to totally individualize, and yet, we're totally connected to everyone else. How does that work?"

"Sometimes it seems that thoughts come out of nowhere – do they?"

"Karma is everything that's happened to you up to this point. You have to let everything go– the good and the bad. That's where the work is."

"This whole trip certainly feels real, and yet at the same time, it is unreal. How does that work? The thing is, we have to go through the unreal to the next reel."

Doctoring the Doctors

Sometimes Bawa would have the Fellowship doctors come into his room. Many doctors who were in the Fellowship at that time, often ten or more, would come to sit in on his discourses. Bawa would tell us that the thing that really heals the patient is love. He would say that love would directly affect the course of an illness and that we had to be patient ourselves and put our total trust in God in terms of the outcome of the illness for any given patient. In fact, if it was the destiny of the patient to become worse or even to die, then we had to be able to accept that.

He was very concerned about the potential arrogance of doctors and continuously tried to show us that more was going on than we could see. And that's why we had to have a great deal of faith.

"Prayer is something you give to yourself. It's a gift. And you can do it any way you want."

"Own your own story and then disown it … see how that feels."

"Don't look up for God, look in."

"Sometimes it's better to not know about something. We don't always have to fill our head with a lot of stuff we don't need to know— for now anyway."

"To have firm conviction and to be able to surrender— that's a strong combination. However, don't let your convictions make a convict out of you."

House Calls

Sometimes people who were ill in the Fellowship would report that, while they were confined to their beds at home, Bawa would come and visit them while he was continuing to remain at the Fellowship. Usually these visits were to comfort the patient and relieve them of fear.

Sometimes people who were ill thought they were being punished by God because they had not upheld what they considered the right behavior. Bawa said this was nonsense and that the illness in essence was serving as a learning tool, because the only way to go through the illness was with patience, certitude, determination and gratitude.

So people might say, "Well, why would you have gratitude for illness?" Bawa would say, "The illness has come to serve you, and to bring out these qualities of patience and gratitude and faith."

"Too much thinking can make a person ill at ease."

"Everyone has a part in the play– especially little children."

"Don't make a big deal out of a small deal– and you know everything is s small deal. Nothing is a big deal."

"Certainty actually often hides fear."

"A wife can give you strife. A wife can act like a knife, and a wife can help you have a good life. And the same goes for husbands."

Bawa, the Traffic Cop

Sometimes Fellowship people would be disappointed because they wanted to see Bawa heal the person, and to some effect heal them right there. But he didn't work like that. He knew where that person had to be at that time. Sometimes he said, "I'm just like a policeman. I ask you where you want to go, and if I'm going in that direction, I will tell you to wait here, and then I will take you there."

So that's an image of Bawa I've always had; of Bawa as a policeman directing people. My experiences, especially in the early days, were like that. I felt that I was being directed and it was my intention to let myself be directed by those events which seemed to lead me into a more peaceful state.

"It's not that the scene which is unfolding for you is out there– it's coming from in here."

"Everything, everything that you experienced up to this point is gone– gone– so go on."

"Listen– don't give yourself a hard time."

"There are many aspects of ourselves. Which ones we reveal to ourselves is entirely up to us. To reveal this is a process of self-revelation."

"Remember, your history is a total mystery. Sometimes it seems that a lot is happening in a short period of time– and, sometimes it seems that nothing is happening for a long period of time– it's the same thing."

"What the world considers valuable is often not as valuable as what the world considers not valuable."

The Value of Illness

Once when I was in Ceylon, I got what was called Dengue Fever. For three or four days I just felt like I wanted to die because I was so ill. Bawa said, "Good, this will help you to cleanse your body." So his view of things was entirely different than the standard view of Western medicine. This was something that Bawa would say at times.

Bawa worked very hard to get us to not be afraid of illness or death. He wanted us to see it as a part of our life process, and that we needed to trust that process. Whatever was given to us, Bawa wanted us to realize it was given because we needed to have that experience.

"Be fearless, why not? You have nothing to lose except fear, which isn't yours anyway."

"Deep down everyone is really good. It's just that sometimes people forget that they are that good."

"It's all right to change your mind about a situation, even if it's in mid-course, without fear that you're missing something. You know, if you're not there, it's not happening for you at that time. All you're doing is changing direction."

"You could lead your life as if the whole world is watching you on TV, or you could lead your life as if no one is watching you– same thing."

"Life presents some very interesting situations. When you're in the middle of a jam, you're not thinking, "Oh that's interesting." You're thinking, "How am I going to get through this one?"

Ceylon

When I was in Ceylon in 1974 with Bawa one day, we were just sitting in the Ashram. I think Bawa may have been getting a haircut or something. I was sitting in the back of the compound, and there weren't many people there.

Now at the time I had a friend named Skip who was planning to come over to Ceylon and join Bawa. I was sitting in the back and I was writing a letter to Skip telling him not to come because it was too confining there. We hardly ever went out and the teaching was going on all the time.

So I'm writing this letter to Skip giving him reasons why he shouldn't come, and all of a sudden Bawa calls my name and asks me what I'm doing. I tell him, "I'm writing to Skip." Bawa says, "Aw, writing to your friend, complaining about being here?" And then he proceeded to read me the letter I was writing. In other words, he knew what was on the paper that I had written, even though he didn't have the paper in his hand.

He knew many times about how things were, even when it appeared he was at a distance from the thing. It was almost like a part of him was somewhere else even though he was sitting in the same place.

Bawa was kind of like a jungle teacher. It was amazing being with Bawa in this environment. But on the other hand, it was difficult for me to be there because I felt overly confined.

"You never know what you're going to learn about a situation beforehand. Humility is a powerful tool on the path to greater humility."

"It's easy when we're just doing what's in front of us, without judging ourselves."

"You don't always have to say what's on your mind. You can keep it to yourself for the time being. That's called patience."

"If you don't like what's playing, change the channel."

"Men and women relate and understand things differently!"

At the Movies

Once, we were in Bawa's room and there wasn't much going on and he said, "What should we do?" I thought, tell us a story. He said, "I don't have any stories. One of you tell a story." He asked me to tell a story. Well my mind went totally blank. He said, "Come on, come on. We're waiting. Tell us a story." Still I couldn't come up with a story and then he said, "Tell the story. Begin, you're keeping us waiting."

When he said begin, it was like I was in a movie. He said to me, "Tell us what's happening," and I described a situation that was taking place. It seemed that it was a long time ago. I believe it involved the prophets– I don't remember the exact context now, but it was like it was unrolling like a movie and I was there watching it.

Afterward, I described the scene and he responded, "Where did you get that story?" I told him that I had seen it. He said, "That's right, that's how it comes." And then he proceeded to tell the rest of the story and what it meant.

"The best you can do is to take care of your life. No one is going to do it for you."

"Everything that has happened to us up to this point is, in a sense, our history, yet it's a total mysterious mystery. How can we diffuse the emotions? We do this by taking away the devotion to drama. All drama leads to more karma. Don't be a karma farmer. "

"Everyone has their own fears and their own way of dealing with those fears. Don't get mixed up in someone else's fears– deal with your own fears."

"Did you ever leave a scene and wonder, "What was that all about?""

"Did you ever have a conversation with different parts of yourself? Try it. It can be fun. You never know what you have to say to yourself."

The Monk Story

When Bawa was in Ceylon in the '70s, a Buddhist monk came to see him. The monk was an American who had been in the jungles of Ceylon for eight years. He came to Bawa in his robes and presented himself. Bawa took his hand to greet him. The monk, who later became my friend, told me that when Bawa greeted him, he felt electricity going through his entire body. He continued to feel like that for the next three days. This monk has a very strong character and related many stories to me about his time in India.

At one point, he was at the Ganges River and he watched the rituals going on. One of the rituals was that people would immerse themselves in the Ganges and drink water from the river. This was in an area where bodies were being cremated, people were washing their clothes, and people were relieving themselves. Everything was going on in that river, which included dead animals floating down the river. My friend saw this scene and said to himself that he could never drink the water of the Ganges. But then he decided to venture. Once he was in the water, an incredible sense of peace came over him and he immersed himself in the water and drank some of the water of the Ganges. He never got ill from that experience.

This is a story about letting go. My friend was so

committed to experiencing these things of the people around him, that he gave up all his ideas about disease and germs and let himself go into that experience without fear.

"Listen, do yourself a favor. If you ask someone about something such as, "How are the kids," make sure you really want to know."

"It's hard to trust our own decisions, but we have no options. We have to do that in order to be all right with ourselves."

"The idea is to get your life to where it is doable, manageable, and somewhat in order."

"Don't carry the world around, or your history around like a burden. In fact, don't carry them around at all."

"Some people think and say that we came here to suffer. Hmmmmmmm. I don't think so."

Things Can Change Fast

On a particular morning, I was sitting in the Mosque, and at one point I sort of went out to another dimension and was in another scene which involved a group of men just standing around talking.

At one point, while I was in this scene, someone spoke to me. I was just about to respond when I was back in the Mosque and I realized instantly that what I had to say came from another scene that I had just taken part in. So I didn't say what was on the tip of my lips since I was sitting in the Mosque. This was very quiet and serene and what I had to say out loud would have nothing to do with what was going on at that moment at the Mosque.

"Everyone and everything comes into our life at exactly the right time."

"Every once in awhile, give yourself a real compliment. What the hell, why not?"

"Relaxing is hard to do at times. Worrying and agitation are even harder on the body and mind."

"And sometimes just think, "I have nothing to do with any of this … I'm just an actor myself.""

"When you're by yourself you can act as mature as you want, or as silly as you want– it makes no difference."

The Power of Prayer

We all have our own relationship to what is going on within ourselves. Sometimes this comes in dreams, or in a vision, which is like a waking dream. Now I've been doing these Five Times prayers pretty regularly lately. Last evening, I went to bed and I had not done the last prayer of the day. I thought, "Oh, too late." I was tired. So I went to bed at 9:00 p.m. A half hour later, I was summoned awake. There was a presence in the room. Bawa appeared to be like a sergeant in the army. It seemed to be that he was doing a bed check and he came up to me and touched me and said, "Up," and now I'm up, sitting up. So I went ahead and said the last prayer of the day. Then I went back to sleep. So what was that all about? There is a power in prayer. It's for us to experience it. Now I had many experiences of this nature at the beginning of my relationship with Bawa.

Bawa had asked us to get up at four in the morning to pray. Most people found this very difficult to do. I seemed to hone in on it as a good practice and I took it up and had committed to do it. What would happen sometimes, and it happened quite frequently, is that just about at four a.m. there would be a knock at my window, a bird would start singing, I would feel a knock on my head, I would hear bells ringing, I would hear my name in my own voice, or the voice of a female. Sometimes the clues are that clear.

So this business of getting up early in the morning at that time for me has been a major part of my life.

"Why is it that churches and religions and that whole gang behave as if they have got the whole God knowledge down? I mean what kind of arrogance is that?"

"Childhood can be a scary experience, depending on who is doing the caring and how daring the caring."

"When you really, really master the art of being alone – you can then really be alone with others."

"It's all a dream, until we realize that it is all a dream. Until then, we need to participate in the dream as if it were real … if we choose."

The Three-Piece Suit Story

This is a story about an experience which I had after Bawa passed away. I had started giving the call to prayer at the Mosque several times a week. Of course I had great trepidation about doing this, because I can't sing at all, and this seemed to be a really important thing to do. I had no training to do this, which is essentially to play the role of the muezzin, or the person chosen to give the call to prayer at the Mosque. So one evening I had this kind of vision while I was sleeping. A group of us are sitting around Bawa. Bawa was leading us in song and kept taking the notes higher and higher. We were sort of chanting and I could feel myself beginning to be absorbed in that sound which we were making. This went on for awhile and I opened my eyes and there was only Bawa and myself. He was very tall, and dressed in a dark, three-piece suit. He told me, "Yes, you can do this. You can be successful. That's what you do." And that was the experience with Bawa which I've held on to. In essence, he was showing me that I could be successful in this world. I've held onto that one because it was kind of a benchmark experience with Bawa for me.

"Don't do things because you think you ought to– do them because you want to."

"Do what you gotta do– see what happens."

"Everything on the planet receives life from one source– isn't that amazing? Our purpose here is to go to that source, and use that gift, for the good of everyone."

"Be your own independent film channel."

"A big part of wisdom is to learn which situations to get involved in, or not get involved in– it really is as simple as that."

The Secret Storm

In the early days, there was a TV soap opera called the "Secret Storm." Bawa would say to us, "Secret Storm," and he would indicate to us that our lives were just like the Secret Storm. There was a whole issue with how much English he understood. He came from the jungles. When he first came, he would read the Dick and Jane books.

I'm telling this because sometimes he would be speaking, and would stick in a phrase. He'd say, "Knife, wife." He'd tell a story then – like if you didn't treat a woman right, she could be like a knife.

After a while you didn't have to say anything to him– he would know what you had to say. Sometimes he would tell you what you were thinking. He could tell you a story about what you were thinking.

"As we change, the world also changes. It's like that. The world isn't what we think it is. There is no objective reality."

"No matter how you look at it, we're here on our own. We're on our own journey on this trip as far as we can see."

"There really is only one fear. It's just broken down into many little fears. The one fear is that we can't handle our fears. That's why we have them, to go through them."

"The world can seem like a prison or a prism. It's our choice."

"You never know what the way will bring. Sometimes we have to lose the connection to someone in order to regain the connection to someone. That makes things more interesting anyway, since each someone will not be the same, and the connection will also not be the same. Actually, we can do this with all aspects of our life."

The Five Minute Story

One Saturday I was at home with Anne, who was my wife at the time. I said to her, "Why does Bawa tell such long stories? Why doesn't he just give us a five-minute discourse? Then we can all go home." Well, she laughed. Then that evening we were at the Fellowship. Now it was always a big deal to have Bawa speaking on a Saturday. There was a big crowd. Bawa would wait until the people had showed up and he would then decide to come down the stairs to the group. This was almost like a scene from a movie– his presence was so powerful.

He started coming down the stairs. I was standing against the wall so that I could greet him. So he walks up to me, looks me in the eye, and says to me, "You! Go downstairs and speak for five minutes." Now this was a big deal to speak before Bawa spoke. It was sort of like being the opening act for a big performer. When he said that, I totally tripped out, because now I became the focus.

Now I'm sitting on the stage, Bawa is sitting behind me, a little bit higher. I have the microphone in front of me. To this day, I have no idea of where the words came from that I spoke. I think it had something to do with the value of being in the Fellowship. Anyway, after five minutes he said, "Ok, that's very good," and he picked up the story that I had begun.

That experience was so powerful for me because I had to really let go in a sense, because that amount of attention was put on me and there, right behind me, is the Guru watching and listening. It was an archetypical type of scene for me, like this was all happening somewhere else.

Now if I really think about it, this entire journey with Bawa has been, and continues to be, a journey through time.

"What can you say about religions? The less, the better! Practice your own religion if you need one, to lead your life fully knowing all the time that death is right beside you. That's leading your life fully. If you must have a religion, please make it one without the fear of God."

"It's a great paradox: when we go deeper and deeper into that feeling of being totally alone here on this planet, we allow ourselves to also be totally at one with everyone and everything."

"How can you know what's going to happen when it hasn't even happened yet. There is no future. It's all a projection from the moment."

"The thing is to want nothing, absolutely nothing. That's how we become free."

"Sometimes you think and feel that you can't possibly go on. Keep going, what the hell, why not? At least the trip is interesting–if you make it interesting."

Letting Go of the Guru

Now in early 1986, Bawa was getting progressively worse in terms of his health. He was confined to his room and the general feeling was that he was seriously ill, and that we really should not bother him unless it was absolutely necessary. So I stayed away a great deal.

Then, in October of that year I was at the Fellowship House and Bawa told the group of us that the only reason he was staying around was because of the attachment of the children, and that we really had to start letting him go. He also indicated that once he left his body, he could do a lot more work and be more available to us. At that point, I realized that we owed that to him, to let go."

"Did you ever watch a smoke ring and how it disappears? That's like our thoughts. They disappear in the same way."

"Things look one way and then they look another way."

"Be flexible– it helps to unflex those parts of us that need unflexing."

"Listen, ultimately we have to let go of all attachments. I mean all attachments."

"Accepting the role that others want us to play is fine, as long as we're fine with it."

Epilogue

Life is a secret within a secret. Our work here is to keep journeying into the secret, then it won't be a secret anymore.

The Fellowship has continued now for over 40 years. It continues to be an extremely important aspect in many peoples' lives. To me, it's kind of a magical theatre where anything can take place. Whatever you take there as an intention is what you will receive. Bawa was a powerful force when he was here. He's even a more powerful force to me now that he's gone over.

"People talk of the Sufi way. Wrong.
If there is a way, it's not Sufism."

About the Author

After receiving his doctorate in psychology in 1969, Dr. Art Hochberg proved himself to be a dynamic teacher and innovator in the field of psychology. Within a year of receiving his degree, he became the Psychology department head at St. Mary's College in South Bend, Indiana, and also taught at Notre Dame University where he initiated several new courses and program changes toward the field of Humanistic Psychology. Dr. Hochberg was one of the earliest members of the Association for Humanistic Psychology, and gave several talks on the subject at their annual conference.

While continuing to develop his own ideas in the field over the next nine years, he taught experientially-oriented psychology courses, travelling in Uganda, Ceylon, Israel, and Switzerland, among other countries. All the while, he was deepening his spiritual focus. He visited religious centers, spent a year in a Zen Buddhist monastery and has spent thirty-nine years studying with the Sufi Master Bawa Muhaiyaddeen.

Dr. Hochberg's vision was transformative on an organizational level as well. Wherever he worked, it was common for him to revamp the institution's existing program, hire new staff, and take part in presenting the new program to the general public. Such examples in the late 70's include Urbana College in Ohio where he was the Division Chairman of Social Services; in Fort Dix, NJ, where he was the Clinical Director of the Drug and Alcohol Program, supervising 20 drug and alcohol counselors, developing treatment programs for the patients at Walson Army Hospital, and conducting seminars around the base for commanders, soldiers, and their dependents. In 1979 at the newly established Fordham-Page Clinic in Radnor, PA, Dr. Hochberg served as Clinical Director, responsible for counselor training, teaching nutrition, and presenting the clinic's holistically-oriented program to the public.

In the early 80's, Dr. Hochberg established his private practice. In the early years of his practice, he was known as a nutritional psychologist, since he was one of the few psychologists in the country at that time using nutrition in their practice. He appeared on television and was a radio guest numerous times speaking about the nutritional approach to the treatment of psychological problems. Several national magazines and newspapers also covered his groundbreaking work. He trained under such notable practitioners as Dr.

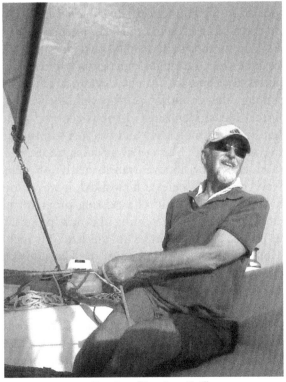

Dr. Art, "Letting Go!"

Paavo Airola, a Finnish Nutritionist; Dr. John Christopher, a leading herbalist; and Dr. Carl Pfeiffer, who was the foremost orthomolecular psychiatrist at the time. Dr. Hochberg joined the International Academy of Preventive Medicine and spoke at several medical conferences about the role of Psychology and the body, appearing with Dr. Linus Pauling, and Dr. Jeffrey Bland, among others.

In addition, Dr. Hochberg had a practice at the Center for Preventive Medicine in Bala Cynwyd, Pennsylvania for eleven years, and published fifteen articles on stress and nutrition. In November, 1981, Prevention Magazine wrote a feature article about his work on nutrition as he combined it with Psychology which was included in Prevention's Complete Book of Vitamins in 1984. Dr. Hochberg also wrote a chapter in *The Metabolic Management of Cancer — A Physicians Protocol and Reference Book.* In 1993, he became the Director of the Holistic Health Program at Rosemont College in PA, and was also on the Adjunct Psychology faculty at Widener University. He also worked as a prison psychologist in southern New Jersey, and in several outpatient mental health clinics in New Jersey and Pennsylvania.

Currently, Dr. Hochberg continues to maintain his own private practice as a licensed psychologist, and mainly deals with the transformational process that people can experience as they go through the various "changes" in their life. These "changes" serve as the Process for each individual's transformation, and greater self-awareness. In addition, Dr. Hochberg serves as an intake psychologist at a Philadelphia inner city mental health clinic. He has written several articles and pamphlets on Transformational Psychology, a term which he coined, which transcends the scope of Transpersonal Psychology by addressing the core issues of our human existence as they are reflected in our daily spiritual life.

Other Dr. Art Books

Lightin Up! *Healing Through Passion and Humor,* Second Edition

The issues of our life have within them the seeds of spiritual awareness. With *Lightin Up!: Healing Through Passion and Humor,* Dr. Art Hochberg gives us a collection of aphorisms that nurture that kind of awareness. They effectively redirect our focus inwards and encourage us to let go of what we think we know, so that genuine and lasting self-discovery can take place. In a very accessible format, the author's wise, sometimes humorous promptings can be read from cover to cover, or at random; each of them inspiring us to:

- Courageously discover our individuality by deciding to be who we really are
- Experience the aliveness which fuels our creativity
- Recognize and go with what is happening for us
- Be spiritual in whatever we do
- Stay out of other people's take on reality
- Allow each day to be a lifetime of learning

We are all here for a supreme purpose — to experience the exaltedness of our human birth.

Available in print and eBook formats at Amazon, Barnes & Noble, Lulu, and the Apple iBookstore.

Letting Go *or A Practical Guide to Throwing Out the Garbage*

Dr. Art Hochberg offers his time-tested, "Letting Go"— your medicine kit of ten emotional remedies to stay sane and free of disabling fear and worry. When you're ready to change, Dr. Art's aid works with your own inner voice of wisdom to guide you on your personal journey of self-discovery.

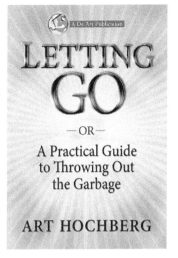

Dr. Art's heartfelt "Letting Go" remedy for daily life shows how easily we can feel contentment and how difficult and exhausting it is holding onto old hurts, grief, losses, resentments and sadness. Learn to win in your life by letting go of pain and opening your heart.

The Dr. Art "Letting Go" recipe has been tested and shared by counselors, teachers and mental health professionals. Share the healing secret of "Letting Go" with your friends and family.

"Dr. Hochberg provides an alternative to conventional Psychology and Medicine ... for stress related complaints such as depression and anxiety." —Prevention Magazine

"He is a definite force in the field of psychology." —Philadelphia Magazine

Available in print and eBook formats at Amazon, Barnes & Noble, Lulu, and the Apple iBookstore.

Made in the USA
Middletown, DE
21 August 2023